Towheaded Stone Thrower

Also by Jim Peterson

Poetry
The Man Who Grew Silent
An Afternoon with K
The Owning Stone
The Bob and Weave
Original Face
Speech Minus Applause
The Horse Who Bears Me Away

Poetry Chapbooks
Carvings on a Prayer Tree
Jim Peterson's Greatest Hits
The Resolution of Eve

Fiction
Paper Crown (novel)
The Sadness of Whirlwinds (short stories)

Plays
The Shadow Adjuster
Beholder (also a short film)
Ruby Cat and Mister Dog (two monologues for women)
The Falling Man
Seeing Purple

TOWHEADED STONE THROWER

THE HARRIET POEMS

JIM PETERSON

Press 53

Winston-Salem

Press 53, LLC
PO Box 30314
Winston-Salem, NC 27130

First Edition

SILVER CONCHO POETRY SERIES
edited by Pamela Uschuk and William Pitt Root

Cover art, "Untitled," Copyright © 2024 by Chris Cohen
Used by permision of the artist

Cover title design by Grant Kittrell

Author photo by Paul Kayhart

Library of Congress Control Number
2024951829

ISBN 978-1-950413-89-8

For Harriet

(1951-2016)

.

After her death, three Post-it notes in Harriet's handwriting
were found on her desk:

The birds sang at the break of day,
Start again I heard them say,
Don't dwell on what has passed away
Or what is yet to be

—Leonard Cohen

Anyone can slay a dragon, he told me, but try waking up
every day and loving the world all over again.

—Brian Andreas

Always saddle your own horse.

—Connie Douglas Reeves

Personal Thanks

With the deepest love and gratitude I want to thank the people who showed up for Harriet during her illness, who came to the house and spent various kinds of time with her when she needed it the most: Peggy Hardin and Janet Raffetto, Moh Hardin and Cynde Grieve, Wannie and Betsy Hardin, Charlotte Wiley, Camille Alexander, Caitlyn Bradley, Elizabeth Narehood, LuAnn Keener-Mikenas, Nancy Allen, Joyce Abbott, Scott Walter, Lysa Slay, Liz and Gary Dop, Julie Hemstreet and David Schwartz, Kathy Schaefer, Carol Goldman, John Abel, Laura-Gray Street, Tobie and Kenny Bentz, Joyce Martin Brown, Nell Jenkins, Susan Todd, Greg and Dawn Turner, the Nataraja Women's Drum Ensemble, all of Harriet's dressage and eventing students and friends . . . and many more whose names escape me in this moment for which I sincerely apologize. She gave a lot to others in her life. Thank you for giving so much love back to her when she needed it most. And if you didn't show up personally, that's okay too. If you knew her, you loved her, and she could always feel the presence of that love, those good vibes. Much love and gratitude to you too.

A special thanks to the following poets: Rebecca Rotert for her encouragement on the earliest draft of this manuscript. Ellen Doré Watson for her reading and tough critique of this manuscript in a later phase. Fred Arroyo, Tami Haaland, and Bill Trowbridge for their readings of the manuscript in the late stages. Steve Corey for his insightful reading of "What You Left Behind in the Silent House." Grant Kittrell, Patricia Henley, Marya Hornbacker, and Chris Gaumer for their very helpful critiques of individual poems.

I also want to thank the editors of The Silver Concho Poetry Series, Pam Uschuk and William Pitt Root, for selecting this book. Finally, my sincere gratitude goes to Kevin Watson for his work on the design and interior layout of this collection and for all that he does for Press 53 writers.

—Jim Peterson

Acknowledgments

Many of these poems published in the following journals, anthologies, and collections appeared in earlier versions:

Cave Wall: "Woodcreek 1977," "The Prisoner's Dance," "The Last Horse"

The Good Life Review: "Bend," "The Hammock"

I-70 Review: "Presence," "Sentence"

I-70 Review: as featured poet: "Allow Everything," "The Hills," "Banana Pudding," "The Feather," "The Minutes"

James Dickey Review: "All at Once," "No Wonder" (as "Come Back"), "Gone," "The Scheme"

A Literary Field Guide to Southern Appalachia: "Two of Them"

Poem: "Near"

Rattle: "Following You," "Everything" (as "The Light")

South Dakota Review: "Open House," "What You Left Behind in the Silent House"

South Dakota Review: "Kissing Harriet," "Planting a Tree," "Riding a Bike," "Pyramids," and "The Banished" under the one title "Some Versions of Harriet"

Southern Poetry Review: "Whirlpool"

Sugar House Review: "Eye to Eye," "Indication"

Whetstone: "What You Showed Me" (as "The Power")

Some of the poems herein appeared in different versions in the following previous collections:

"What You Showed Me" as "The Power" in the *Bob and Weave* (Red Hen Press, 2006)

"Woodcreek 1977" and "The Prisoner's Dance" in *Original Face* (Gunpowder Press, 2015)

"Whirlwind" in *Speech Minus Applause* (Press 53, 2019)

"Open House" in *The Horse Who Bears Me Away* (Red Hen Press, 2020)

Contents

Prologue

One: *What You Showed Me*

Two: *Ice Moon Days*

3. *The Banishment of With and Without*

Epilogue

Prologue

Towheaded Thrower of Stones

Mid-way up an oak beside the old house
a towheaded girl sits on a muscular limb
and throws stones. She gathered them
for weeks in the nearby woods because they
spoke to her, at first from under fallen leaves,

then from the hard ground of the trail,
and finally from her bedside-table box deep
in the night, telling her how high and far
and what direction. The stones were tired
of tumbling in the white-water creek

at the bottom of the steep hill behind
her house, tired of staring at wild-eyed
weasels on the forest floor, of being kicked
up and down the trails like empty tin cans.
She holds a stone in her hand, turns it

to see its many faces. It tells her it wants
to fly like a hungry ghost in the blackest night
and land in the midst of anything it's never
been. Wants to be a seagull diving for shifty
mackerel in the wave, wants to be a leaf-cutter

lugging its green cargo over the forest floor.
Another wants to stumble drunk
and voracious into grimy grocery store
parking lots, grinning with some unstoppable
inner fire. One wants to be a gravedigger working

in a hole so steep he can't climb out, so cold
he can't feel his hands on the shovel. One
slender stone of multiple shades of blue and gold
wants to be a woman striking the rawhide
goatskin of a djembe for her dancing sisters

or even a politician rousing the angry crowd.
One square gray stone rolls in her palm like a die,
says it wants to be a skinny boy playing his flute
alone on the street where strangers stop to listen.
One wants to be a woman in a tank top eating

peaches over a pan. Another to make love, to bear
children sharp and beautiful as diamonds.
The final stone has no fear of life, death, or relatives—
though there are many—no fear of boulders
and sand, or the zeal of steel-headed hammers.

But no one can say this stone doesn't love, having
descended from some unimaginable wholeness,
broken, blasted, battered, thrown into some far
corner of the world by a towheaded child.
That night in her bed, empty box now silent

on the table, the girl detects the rough voice
of this last thrown stone, coming to her from
so far away she can barely remember
its scarred face. Your grief is my grief,
it whispers, and never speaks again.

One: What You Showed Me

All at Once

for Harriet at Woodcreek Lake, Summer of 1970

When it started raining harder,
tiny eyes on the surface
blinked as if the lake itself
were waking up. Everyone

but the two of us—even your
current boyfriend—went
scrambling and laughing
to the house and a stack

of big fluffy towels. You and I
ducked under the dock, the rain
reduced there to rows of dribbles
from the cracks between slats

above us. Wet is wet, I said,
trying to be clever. You laughed,
rain drops streaming down
your cheeks. We reached up between

the boards above us and hung there,
face to face, up to our necks
in the lake. We didn't miss
your boyfriend one bit, or any

of the others for that matter.
I saw clearly that you wanted me
to want you, and I did—all day
with accidental touches, glances

that lasted a second too long.
Your yellow bikini shone like two
exotic fish beneath the surface.
Our words said absolutely nothing

and everything. Wet is wet meant
I felt that we were one
with the lake surrounding us,
that the lake was one

with the woods surrounding it,
that the woods were one
with the sky surrounding them,
that the sky was one with the unknown—

all at once. Eye to eye, for the first
time not compelled by shame
to look away. Your boyfriend called
your name from the screened porch,

his voice drifting like a breeze far out
on the lake. In that moment we both
saw it—you in me and me in you.
We knew that we knew what we knew.

Following You

I followed you up the face
of that cliff-riddled mountain.
I am tall, stiff, scared of heights.

You are small, lithe, quick and not
scared of anything in the physical
world. At first the easy handholds

and footholds gave me confidence.
But narrow ledges curving under
overhangs began to take their toll.

I stalled, my face pressed to rock,
no way forward or back. The fall
was steep for three hundred feet,

then a sloped field of boulders, then
the tops of firs rising towards us.
You coached, guided my hand

to a hold I couldn't see, and suddenly
I could swing around to you.
We grew silent in our climbing

as the sun beat down on us hot
and the wind whipped us cold.
You led the way, finding routes

that only a lizard would see. The top
was faraway above us and out
of sight. I kept my eyes straight

ahead on the rock, feeling
for the next hold. Or I watched
the soles of your feet, your

swaying butt, the braid of your long
blond hair swinging back and forth.
On a steeper, more difficult face

you kept describing finger holds,
but when I reached they felt like
band aids stuck to the stone.

Still, I made the next ledge again
and again. The shadows of hawks
and eagles flashed across me as if

I'd become stone myself. I could
hear your words, but I didn't listen.
Wind whistled and whispered across

the countenances of great cliffs.
A hawk's fractured cry scattered down
the valley of crags and spires.

I watched the wavy shadow-feet
of clouds as if they knew the way
home. Your voice fell on me

from above like my own thoughts,
saying to keep reaching and feeling,
to keep moving. And I did, managing

somehow to trust the sliver of an edge
to pull myself up to you. We sat
for hours on that ledge, our bodies

fused at hip and shoulder. The vastness
swirled and thickened. Our eyes
and ears traveled so far into the unknown,

we could barely breathe.

What You Showed Me

1.

Wind cannot penetrate the long hall
of horses. We feel nothing but the weight
of their silent response, see nothing
but the scars of leftover moonlight.
We hear nothing but the soft plunk
of our feet in the stray oats and straw
and the drowsy arising of giants.
The switch on the wall brings light
and down both sides of the barn
their long sleepy faces emerge.
I lead the big stallion outside,
his curious lips nibbling my ear,
tack him up quickly by starlight,
ask him for a trot which he gives
over the dirt road and through the pines.
The cup of an ear pricks back to listen.
The mind falls down into his haunches,
my legs the subtle-shifting root nerves
of both our bodies. My hands collect
the weight of each hoof thrusting
and falling, calling the four beats
to the three beats of the canter.
My butt glides as one with the calm
center of the black leather saddle,
pushing his body against the steady
contact of my hands with the steel bit
that splits the back of his mouth.
The limbs cut in above and beside me.
I ride with my face to the mane,
his head lunging down and out
as he gathers himself to launch us
through a long climbing tunnel of trees
till we spring into the field of light
and into the flow of young slash pines
that slant to the west in a low groundswell

of darkness around and beneath me.
Galloping your long-legged mare
behind me, you draw neck and neck
beside me on the trail. We reach out
as before, our hands entangled in the air
between us as all things grow together
in the speeding darkness around us,
the power flowing from beneath us,
churning the earth back behind us,
your face a mask of moonlight and leaves.
I cannot feel you apart from the knot
of our hands suspended between us.
These animals know where they're going.
No voice could shatter this stillness.
A stand of trees rises before us
and a broad path cuts through them
like a private peeling back of the waters
that bears us into swirling configurations
of fireflies overwhelming the night.

2.

For the sake of our horses we must rest.
I follow the fork to the pond and dismount.
His ears flop like an old mule's in the wind.
Twin plumes of mist explode from his nostrils.
I can hear my blood still charging
from heart into brain and back again.
I can hear the wind sidling up to branches
and the close stamping of hooves,
the sucking of moonstruck water
into the great living barrels of bodies.
Wind-ripples flash on the surface.
The golden trail glows like an arm
of the moon reaching down to us.
Hoofprints darken into craters.
I watch you standing beside me,
long reins looped down from your hand
to your horse's head grazing in grass.
You turn to me, your face half shadow,
half shining, your blond hair mingling
with bay mane, the miraculous oval
of your one visible eye, full of me.

Bend

I found you walking beside a horse
without halter or lead. It shadowed you,
sometimes resting its enormous head
on your shoulder. I'd been alone
for a long time. I feared you were the end
of all that. Sometimes at night
we laid a blanket down in the pasture,
the dark, ground-hugging clouds of horses
grazing around us. I talked a lot
but you didn't care. You were already
who you were. When a horse saw you
its ears pricked forward. Its eyes
followed you. When the horse stumbled
and fell, it was you who stumbled and fell.
When it flew over the fences and creeks
it was you flying. When its body curved
from nose to tail, when it shortened
or stretched out its gait, it was you.
I said teach me. You showed me my hands
that didn't know they were feeling
the horse in the reins. You showed me
my legs and feet that didn't know
they were shaping the stream of that body.
I couldn't fathom that my thoughts
fell into the river of the horse and altered
its course, its bearing. As I learned, I felt
the current of my body bend
toward the current of yours. Their confluence—
woman, man, and horse walking together.

Eye to Eye

on a photograph by Harriet

Holding the camera for a closeup,
you capture your reflection
in the horse's eye.
You are looking out
of the horse's eye
as well as in. And I am looking
at the black-framed photo
into the horse's liquid eye
over the camera pressed
to your face,
past your right shoulder
into the open white barn
down the long aisle to the far blue door
where light and darkness
spin like yin and yang.
On the day you took that picture
the horse swayed
and drifted in his cross ties
like a boat within a slip.
You are the one
who sends your energy deep
into his mind and muscle
and bids him to travel
through gates and fields,
over forest roads and trails,
sun in your eye or behind the ridge,
days full of birds and wind.
I see you in his eye
and I am in there with you,
mountains rising up in their gray-blue grace,
the cloud-riddled sky beyond.
We are everything and nothing
as the horse's eye contains us,
and lets us go.

Woodcreek 1977

A golden retriever named Jason
lies in a pile of red and yellow leaves,
dark eyes ready for more play,
one front paw nonchalantly draped over the other,
happiness penetrating us like air.

A friend loaned us her summerhouse that winter,
the grad student and the riding instructor,
a poorly built fireplace in the main room
all we had for heat, naïve portraits
of the family's long dead horses
all we had for art. There was nothing to believe
or trust, and everything to learn.

The only way to find us
was the long furrow of a road among slash pine.
Nobody came. The moonlight played
in a million spoons on the lake.
The old fishing boat kept untying itself,
drifting out from the ancient boathouse
like a dead leaf. We are the ones who paddled
at midnight among the nibbling bream.

We are the ones who came flying drunk
down the backwoods macadam
on that leaky old motorcycle
held together with green cord and duct tape.

Today I put my ear to the ground and hear
our bodies careening through the underbrush
of that long ago night while the motorcycle spins
on its foot peg and chokes out on sand.

Remember this with me—
you who were there—
the way we lay flat under that pale night sky
scraped and bruised among the scrub oak
laughing at the silence,
laughing at our own dumb luck.

Presence

I flip the switch on the living room lamp.
Everything is still, silent, according
to plan. Small shadows with edges replace
the large shadow that was simply darkness.
And you are here somewhere, not hiding

but hidden in the house, hanging a photo
in a hall, or bending over a partially stained
board in the basement workshop. A shell
flashes on the carpet, first found on the beach
at Chicahauk beside an old steering wheel

that I also picked up and carried home—you
wove it with holly branches and hung it on
the porch. I retrieve the wayward shell and place it
in a jar on the kitchen window sill beside
the painted rock where I know you will find it.

Kissing Harriet

I was kissing Harriet on the neck. It felt so good, I didn't want to stop.

"Don't stop," she said.

So I kept on kissing. Each kiss was a step deeper in. I was on a journey through a forest, a path leading down to a beach at the Outer Banks. It was the end of something, and the beginning of something else. I didn't know what. I tore pieces of bread off the loaf in my hand and tossed them above my head. A cloud of seagulls swarmed around me, plucking each piece out of the air. I wondered if they would devour me when the bread gave out. Their eyes were Harriet's, thousands of them glancing at me, then looking away. I was still kissing her neck.

"I went on a trip to the Outer Banks," I said.

"Me too," she said. "We were sitting on a porch, overlooking the ocean. A great storm stood up on the horizon and started walking toward us. It ripped the clouds with bolts. It made the whole sky growl and spit at us. It flung the cold wind at us, and we laughed. It could tell we loved it. 'Help me,' it said. 'I've got too much of this.' It handed us lightning bolts and we buried them deep in the sand dunes. They lit up like lava lamps."

I was kissing her neck. I moved up to her ear.

"Mmmmm," she said. "Don't stop."

I couldn't stop anyway, so I kept on. I moved to her cheek. To her eye. It was closed. It fluttered under my lips like a moth. To her forehead. To the point of her nose. To her other cheek. To the other side of her neck, a great warm lake with mountains rising up on every side. We were in a canoe, paddling slowly. A huge mother moose stood knee deep in the shallows. She plunged her head into the water and pulled up vegetation from the bottom. She chewed with the sidelong sliding of her jaws. "Good," she said to us, and we nodded. Her baby stood on the shore calling to her impatiently. "Mamamamamamamamamamamamama . . ." I was kissing Harriet's neck.

"I went on another trip," I said.

"Me too," she said. "We were paddling on a lake in the mountains.

A mother moose was feeding from the bottom. She carried her baby on her back. She came over to us and we weren't afraid, though she was as huge as a storm. She nibbled with her nimble lips on the weeds of our hair, but it didn't hurt. Her baby whispered in my ear."

"What did it say?" I asked.

"It said that it belonged to us, but we would never see it again."

I stopped kissing her neck.

"No," she said. "It's okay. It's the way it is. Don't stop."

I started kissing her neck again. I moved up to her face. Her eyes were so close to mine they multiplied like a flock of gulls surrounding me. My hands were full of bread. Her lips parted and her breath came hot and sweet. I started kissing her lips and I knew we were going deeper in.

"This is what we are given," she whispered.

I didn't know what to say, so I just kept kissing her. "Mmmmm," she said. "Don't stop. Don't ever stop."

The Unborn: Two Visions

1

One day long before he was not born my son
set out on a walk. It's hard to imagine him then,
but he was there, and not there, walking
on a trail in the woods I knew well but it was
a first for him, the low fall sun breaking into ribbons
on the forest floor around him. He walked steadily,
but leisurely too, already abandoning everything

he might become. No one knew him yet,
not like the mottled light on his arms
and legs, on his face. His mother and I,
who were already not his mother and father,
spread a soft blanket on a great cold boulder
next to the white-water creek coming down
from the mountain. As we made love

the slanted light lay down and fell asleep
in the leaves. Darkness woke up, climbed out
from beneath the stone, and rose up around us
like a ghost. Stars sputtered through the sparse
fall canopy thrashing in the wind above us. Our son
followed the winding trail all day and night, the wind
tugging him in many directions. He was already

confusing the light with the darkness,
his hands with the leaves, the soles of his feet
with the dome of his head. He was already
not thinking the stale thoughts that would have
bound him to a separate mind for a lifetime.
Instead he was the gray smoke of fox crossing the trail,
the one-eyed rabbit stalk-still in the tall grass.

Long before our son was born and not born, we gathered
our clothes and dressed. The cold wind bit our skin
and the trees made outlandish gestures. We walked
back in the darkness toward a small house with one dim
light in the window, where our son would never
see us, never hear our quiet voices rambling
in its rooms, never address us by our untrue names.

2

My daughter was almost close enough to touch,
her presence balanced on the cusp of two worlds.
She was born inside of a dream that shone around
the bodies of her father and mother like an aura.
She does not exist in this world
where she digs the meat out of words with a spoon.
My daughter fell like a nut from the canopy of a tree
and crawled into the fields and woods beyond,
her skin in the leaves, her voice on the wind.
She has never laid eyes on us though we sit
in the shade of her tree and dream her again and again.
My daughter has never been to a movie,
never sat pressed between two other bodies
while the light coagulates into forms on the screen
but she plays a role in every film we see.
My daughter was almost close enough to touch.
The dream that gave her life also gave her absence.

My daughter lives fully formed in a world
that sinks like a broken bird.
I love her like I love my hands, my eyes,
like breath loves the holes in a wooden flute.
The words of my speechless daughter move in this body
like fish in the currents and eddies of the river.
Like her mother, she throws stones from a tree that fly
into abandoned homes, backyard ponds, crowded
headspaces, faces already full of flesh and bones.
My daughter's hands do not reach out to us
though we feel them on our closed eyes and lips.
She loves us like the wind loves the canopy,
lingering long enough to sing a dying song.
My daughter has never lain in a bed made for her,
house around her sleeping like an invalid dog.
She has never taken a bus or a plane, yet she travels
everywhere with us, the memory of an unfamiliar face.

The Sentence

This morning you walk beneath the undecided trees
in your flowered nightdress. The limbs darken
with russet buds stymied by a final wave of winter.
Your hands, I know, grow numb with reaching high
in the cold air. I make my strong coffee and peel
my boiled egg. I caught a rumor in the store that you
are more than ordinary woman, but I could have told
them that. I shuffle in my slippers from window
to window to watch your progress from tree to bush
to barely risen bulbs. The seamless gray sky contrasts
the hard-earned tan of your face. You stoop to lay your
hand on exposed roots of the cherry tree you planted
ten years ago. I feel your touch on some part of me
called nothing in this particular moment, called
emptiness by some teachers in their books, though it is
something in me that aches and sends me to a chair.
I remove my glasses so I can see both the fuzziness
and the clarity as they come to me in a sentence
without words, the syntax of gain and loss with all
its modifiers coiling and uncoiling in the air between us.

Open House

One Sunday morning we drive
to Famous Anthony's as usual.
I have my regular pancakes,
and you the French toast with bacon.
As we eat, silence gathers
between us like twisted sheets
asking "Is this all there is?"

We look into each other's faraway eyes
and know that this day calls
for the paper's list of open houses.
Here, among the sticky remains
of breakfast, we find the promise
of doors opening to us
at 1 p.m., 2 p.m., 3 p.m., and 4.

We rush home and put
our own house in order.
We dress in fresh jeans
and collared shirts.
We climb into our old Honda
and crank up the radio and the heat.

The 1 p.m. is *a must see to believe.*
We see and we believe— hardwood
floors and ceiling fans, front porch
rockers and a staircase winding to a master
bedroom loft. Looking down on the dark
conversation pit, we know the dog
would struggle with that corkscrew climb,
that we would talk and talk and talk.

The 2 p.m. is *a fixer-upper priced 2 sell.*
Layers of wallpaper, like the rings
of ancient trees, tell the weather
of earlier times, the taste of the long-dead.
We see our future spread before us:
stripping walls, painting, living in a backyard
tent to rip up floors and gut the baths,
to face the ever-changing challenges of tile.

The 3 p.m. is *acreage with a barn*
and fenced pastures. Plateaus
of cow shit harden in the cold wind.
A rusty horseshoe announces each threshold
inside and out. The ranch style house
lies like a closed eye in the treeless pasture.
We sit on a plank of plywood and lean together,
imagining emaciated horses trotting in a ring.

The 4 p.m. is our *dream come true,*
if by dream they mean a studio and a rose garden
and a house that is a universe unto itself.
Weathervanes cruise among the clouds.
Closets reveal hidden stairs and secret wormholes.
Lost in the spiraling galaxy of the third floor
where rooms orbit us like unknown planets,
we have to use our cell phone to call for help.

The winter afternoon is turning dark
as we head home. The silence
that drove us to other houses
transforms to quiet now, hand
in hand above the console.

We park in our driveway and stay
in our seats for a moment, listening
to the wailing of Bob Dylan,
and then to the wind. We savor the call
of warm lights shining in our windows.
Our dog behind the fence grows impatient,
breaks the crystal air
with her abrupt versions of our names.
We have seen enough
from the list of open houses
to know who we are once again,
and who we'll never be.

The Prisoner's Dance

I twist a piece, warm and heavy, from the loaf.
Outside my window, a wren that would fit neatly
in my floating palm, detaches a seed from the feeder

and flits to a bobbing limb of the redbud tree. I remember
the night I would not dance among strangers, even though

her eyes beckoned me to the floor where she stood alone
among the others gathering to the prison of the music.
That's what I called it then in my mind, not understanding

the oiled precision of my own cell. The wren crouches
briefly and uncoils—does she catch the air? or it, her—

where nothing like hope is required. Only weightless feathers
and hollow bones, the desire to leap and fall and swoon,
and blood so quick and light it ends in song. I wrap the bread

in foil and raise my heavy bones from their solid perch.
If I could cradle a willing wren in my hands and carry it

as a gift to the woman standing alone in the yard
speaking in mysterious tongues to the trees she planted,
I know she would shake her head at me and send it

flying on its way. Instead, I quickstep across the threshold
like an old but agile crow. So liberating, now, how she watches me.

Indication

We chose a checkered table
in the soft gray light of a window.
The service slow, you opened your book
about Southerners come to Montana.
I opened my Missoula night-life mystery.

A man walked in holding a little girl
in his arms, small clear-eyed face
below his pointed beard. He stopped
at a table to speak to friends. The child
raised her hand, spoke a continuous lilting

flow of syllables, and they all listened,
father and friends as she held forth,
her face so much like yours in your silent
absorption beside me, blue-gray eyes,
slightest hint of a smile. Somewhere
behind your eyes characters lived out

their lives. When I lay my book aside,
the pages flipped the way an old movie
indicates the passage of time. Layers
of your face separated and shimmered.
I saw the child, straight blond hair

shining, sweetness of the eyes shining.
I saw the old woman, white hair
pressed into the pillow, eyes barely open
and searching, ancient hand reaching
for mine within the bed we share.

Five Snapshots from the Unraveling Road

1

A fallen tree lay bank to bank across the swollen creek
some twenty feet below. Your eyes lit up like fireflies
in a summer twilight. I shook my head and made
fearful noises, but you stepped out on it anyway,
ballerina arms and hands stretched out for balance.
You put on a show for me of almost falling out there
above the fast water laden with boulders. You hopped
to the opposite bank and stood there waiting for me.
I hugged that tree trunk, the muscled water pulsing
under me, and dragged myself across like a snail.
When I reached the other side, you held your hand
out to me, but I made my own way onto my feet,
made my own way down the trail beside the laughing you.

2

We spied a herd of wild horses cavorting on the bluff
above us. I made an illegal u-turn and we headed back,
found the crumbling paved road that switch-backed up
to a desolate parking lot, interpretive signs mangled
or full of bullet holes. We scrambled up a gravelly trail
for a quarter mile, and there they were, fifteen wild horses
frozen mid-gallop, strung out across the rocky, uneven ground
where the Great Grandfather Spirit had cut them loose,
built-up rust on their steel bodies aglow in the sun, the vision
of a Chewelah sculptor. You mounted the largest one,
right hand grasping a shank of mane, Wanapum Lake
bright behind you in the afternoon sun. You gazed at me
from up there, happy and at peace within that arrested fury.

3

We lie on the ground on our backs, slapping our belly-drums
in djembe rhythms. Finally, the curandero calls us into his
healer's hut, a large circular structure beyond the outskirts
of his village. Outside—the calls and scuffles of night time
animals in the Amazon forest. Inside, fire in the center flares up,
smoke pouring out a hole in the roof, the hut otherwise shut
in darkness. The Curandero, also an Ayahuasquero, begins to sing
the sacred songs. His cigarette smoke pulses in coiling waves
above us. In the Curandero's hand, the rattle is so subtle
it can crack your heart wide open. When the cup of ayahuasca
comes, I drink it down. You drink yours down. After the time
of purging is the time of fear, then bliss and visions. Wherever
I go tonight, whatever I see, your hand is here, touching mine.

4

Parked our old, green Chevy van beside the creek. Went to sleep
early in the bed we'd built together. Woke up at dawn to face
the long day of climbing Mt. Katahdin. We passed through deep forest,
scrambled up rocky trails and boulder fields, until we met the steep
ascent switchbacking over the faces of cliffs, exposed now to the wind
and sun. At last we reached the summit of Baxter Peak. Five hours,
four thousand feet of altitude gained. We ate our sandwiches, shared
our crusts with friendly chipmunks. Then we traversed the difficult
Knife Edge Trail to Pamola Peak and began to find our way back down.
Five more hours until we ducked under our stream-washed clothes
on a line hung between two trees. More sandwiches by the creek,
boiled eggs on the camp stove, whiskey with cold beer chasers
from the cooler. Made slow love in the sweetness of that long night.

5

Your arms around me from behind, body snug against my back.
But then you grew tired of my head blocking the world in front of you.
So you bought your own motorcycle, pressed your own face
against the wind. In Nova Scotia, rain battered us, sudden gusts
knocked us sideways, the highway unraveling on the cliffs
above the Bay of Fundy and Northumberton Strait. We ate clams
in Digby, fish sandwiches in Inverness. One hike off the Cabot Trail
brought us face to face with a bull moose, its huge rack opening
like palms to the sky. A trail out of Bay St. Lawrence at the Northern
tip of Cape Breton Island bulged with roots. Art made of found
objects—headless metal torsos, plastic faces, painted animal skulls,
twisted wire feet—hung from the trees. We stopped and stared,
silence heavy in the air. We walked on to the end without looking back.

Planting a Tree

From the window, I could see Harriet planting a tree. She dug the hole in the corner of the front yard fence. A small cherry tree. Its dangling roots reached down when she lowered it toward the hole. She used a small spade to rake the soil back around the roots. The tree's thin branches reached out to hold on to her. She disappeared within them at times as she worked. We have no children, so sometimes I see them where they are not. I walked out into the yard where she had now turned her attention to the small vegetable garden.

"We'll be dead before that tree grows up enough for us to appreciate it," I said.

"Not true," she said.

"And anyway, it's going to grow over the fence and its limbs will dip low and block the path to our front door," I said.

"So what," she said. "We can work on that problem when it happens."

"True," I said, "but you know how cherry trees are: its chest-level limbs will keep me from mowing this whole corner."

"We'll prune as we need to," she said, still pulling up weeds from the garden, swinging her long, blonde braids over her shoulders to keep them out of the way.

"I hope it grows fast," I said, "I want to see it grown and full of blossoms."

"You will," she said, smiling up at me. "Pull some weeds?" she asked.

Just then a neighbor—a tall man with a perfectly bald head—looked over the fence. "What on earth are you folks doing?" he asked.

I didn't like the tone of his voice. "What the hell does it look like we're doing?"

"Haven't you heard?" he said, "the plant exploded."

"What plant are you talking about?" I asked.

"The big one," he said, "and a giant radioactive cloud is heading our way."

Harriet didn't look up from her weeding. "How long do we have?" she asked.

"Ten minutes, maybe less. I've got to go warn the others," he said and disappeared.

"Bullshit," I said.

"Why would he lie?" she asked.

"He's always been a nosy prick," I said.

"That's true." She looked at me, her eyes forgiving my pettiness. "Come kneel down beside me and help me finish the weeding," she said. She patted the grass beside her. I kneeled, my left side pressing against her right one. I peered over the short wire fence around the garden down to where her hands searched out weeds like gentle, vegetarian beasts. In her grip, the weeds let go of the earth and rose to face her eye to eye. She made a big pile on the grass.

Suddenly a huge shadow covered us as a great black cloud slid over the sun. She looked at me and smiled. "Keep weeding," she said, "let's free up the raspberries so they can fly."

"Raspberries don't fly," I said.

"What do *you* call it then?" she asked.

I didn't call it anything, so I couldn't answer, though I wanted to. I wanted to call it flying, but I just couldn't.

I felt a massive but non-threatening presence beside me and I looked over to see the cherry tree growing very fast, its trunk thickening, its big limbs dipping low to the ground then curling up toward the sky, filling with bright pink blossoms, their faint sweetness on the warm breeze, a few pink petals separating and spiraling down to the rain-soaked ground. Its limbs climbed over the fence and dropped so low over the path to our house that visitors would have to plot another route, or else become scramblers. Just as I had predicted. The tree kept groaning in the speed of its growth, blocking out our view of the dark cloud, blocking the doors and scraping the windows of our house with branches and blossoms. Far in the distance, the neighbors were shouting. I couldn't make out their words.

Harriet nudged my side. I turned to look into those grey-blue eyes. "What are you doing?" she asked.

"Watching the tree," I said.

"You're supposed to be helping me," she said.

"Sorry," I said.

The tree wound itself around us until there was nothing but our small space in the yard beside our garden. Harriet was humming happily over her busy hands. I looked up to a hole far above where the black cloud crept. I looked down into the garden and reached in. Beneath my hands, small creatures crawled as if in a vast jungle. "Look," I said, holding the weeds apart for her to see, and she did look—ants transporting their goods, spiders clambering among the blades looking for prey, beetles in search of a partner or friend, a praying mantis holding forth as if to a congregation, my hands hovering over them like the great surround of an ancient tree.

"Another universe," Harriet said. "Many other universes." Then she leaned toward me. "Keep weeding," she whispered. "We have time."

When the weeds were gone, and the raspberries were flying, she took my hand and said "come." We clambered over a limb thick as a man, scuffed our knees on sappy bark and sharp twigs. We climbed through a big, broken window into our living room where the furniture had been talking behind our backs. They snapped to attention and offered their surfaces to us. The dog curled up in her bed and watched over us. Outside our windows: darkness and howling wind. The tree gathered more and more of its mass around our home.

Two: Ice Moon Days

The Ladders Are Flying

On his desktop screen
the surgeon flips through MRI images,
each one the next slice of Harriet's brain,
until at last a moon begins to rise—
white, with a mist of surrounding cirrus—
on some heretofore unimagined
horizon.

*

At first her left hand
wouldn't quite do
what it was supposed to do
when she was drumming
or playing the flute
or holding the reins.

*

Not one of these words
can say what matters.
Each
is a brittle ladder
flying in a void
filled with flying ladders
trying to connect up
or down
or sideways.

The Ice Moon

I don't know why
the ice moon rose
in your brain
bright as a frozen star
on your horizon,
but it did.
I know the moon
reflects light of the sun
but the ice moon is not the moon.
The white-blue ice grows
an inward glacier
freezing out more and more
of who you are.
With each day, each month,
whole continents
in your brain
turn to glaciers,
eerily blue,
contagiously silent,
deeper than the fires
of the sun.
You lie on the couch,
dog sprawled across your legs,
the presence in your eyes
drawn deep within,
lips whispering
of rooms beneath the ice,
landscapes shaped by fire,
whispering again and again
of what you believed was yours forever.

The Hammock

Four a.m., the hammock sways
in the fall breezes, carrying you

through the universe like a great seed pod.
Having abandoned your place in the bed

beside me, you study your pain, your thoughts,
withdrawing into the dark firmament

of the warm cocoon. You ride
the great river of the horse beneath you,

embracing it with your legs,
knowing it in the circle of reins and

heart and mind—the alignment of woman
and beloved beast you manifested day

after day in the fields and forests
and mountain gorges, in the circles

and angles within arenas. The hammock
binds you in that space where your life

rises before you like a colorful breath
and the dew lies down on your face.

New light feels its way through leaves
of the ornamental cherry and the redbud.

You swing between the trees
you planted with your own two hands,

riding that river of a horse down and down
its tortuous course to the ground you must walk alone.

The Last Horse

From the moment we are born, no,
from the instant we are conceived,
that far back, we are dying, but living
too, always both dying and living,
though we forget one or the other
and pretend to ourselves it's only
one: just dying, just living.

I inhale the rich aroma of the horse—
sweat, mud, straw, and manure.
His body sheds white steam in the cold,
his wandering, benevolent eye full
of curiosity. I stand beside Harriet
as she climbs the mounting block
and help her seat her left foot
into the stirrup, then lift her up
onto the saddle and push her right leg
over until she's sitting upright—she
who once sprang into the saddle
with the agility of a gymnast.
No sense remembering or comparing,
unless I want her to feel that blade
of pain, and I don't. But I know
she does feel it. And then she's off,
beginning to remember how to ride,
but now without the strength in her arms
and legs, remembering how to stay
centered over the backbone of the horse,
Tanka, a good old fella with gentle ways
and a long, buckskin winter coat
still streaked with mud from rolling
in the pasture, though we brushed off
as much as we could. She takes him
at a walk, red dust clouds in his wake,
gets him to bend this way and that way.

Then she brings him up to a trot
and I worry—can she stay centered
over him? No, she slips to the left
and begins to slide and her friend
and I run out to hold her up until
we can maneuver her upright
and straight again. Ah, now
she's in the middle, each leg
on a different side of the horse, and she's
enjoying it, but it's taking its toll.
Everything takes a toll. She can feel
the brilliant rider she has always been
still living inside her deep down, that skilled
entanglement with the glorious body
of the great grazer, the magical escape artist.
She feels it, but she can't make it happen
exactly, the signals from her brain
not connecting with her body, or his.
The cold wind kicks up and scatters debris
over the arena's metal roof. The noise makes
Tanka nervous, and he fills with too much
energy, wants to run and buck, evade
the Unknown dancing crazily over his head.
Over her head, too, as she pulls back
on the reins to steady him and draws him
to a halt. She asks to get off, and I help her
swing the right leg over and then slide down
Tanka's flank. Slide down and let go of this
being one with the horse, of teaching others
this art only a few can know, not convertible
to words, how to tune to that wild body
beneath you—it's just happening, no "you"
there at all to interfere or panic or fall.
Whoever is there reading this, please
just erase these words, and maybe

underneath them, she will be there,
hair coming back in black fuzz
over the Frankenstein scar across the top
of her head—hair that once was blond
and long—cheeks now round from the dex,
eyes light blue and so beautiful still, so full
of emptiness and loss that I am dying.
I have to live that dying, hers, and my own.

Allow Everything

I'm here, in my chair beside her on the couch
that has become her home, where sometimes
she faces what she has lost by forgetting
she has lost it. I am learning to allow
everything, because who am I to say no,
or yes. She goes wherever she wants
in the still intact districts of her mind,
a reality I cannot see, or tame with these
words. She plays a tennis match against
Serena Williams at Flushing Meadows,
and holds her own. She jogs five miles
beside the Black Water Creek, seeing an otter
and a Great Blue Heron. She scrambles along
the stunning saddle trail of Mount Katahdin,
unconcerned at how slow I am. She drives
to the barn, grooms and tacks up a horse
named Echo. She mounts. And the earth becomes
her drum, the gathered thundering of hooves.

Riding a Bike

Harriet decides to ride her bike again. She rolls it off the porch, through the gate, and out onto the street. She doesn't look back at the house where her husband watches her from the window. She doesn't want to see the worry in his face. She stands beside her bike, both hands on the handle bars. The connections between her arms and her hands and the bars feel like wings, but flying is not required, only rolling. If she can just do that. But nothing feels right. She doesn't quite know what to do next to get started. She just stands and stares. Why can't she do this? She loves her bicycle. She has ridden it on mountain trails in Montana, on the beaches of the Outer Banks, on winding trails of the Virginia woods, down busy streets to the grocery store or restaurant. She can do this. She reaches her right foot over the center bar and stands over her bike, looking straight ahead down the gentle slope of her street. She won't look at her husband in the window, won't give him any idea that she needs help. She has ridden many miles with no hands, just using slight adjustments of her body to turn, waving with her free hands at the people she passes. She knows how to do this better than most. How can you forget how to ride a bike? She puts her left foot on the left pedal, and pushing with her right foot gets the bike rolling. She places her right foot on the right pedal, and now she is drifting slowly down the street. The air smoothes across her face like cool velvet. She wants to close her eyes and just keep drifting like this forever. But too quickly she reaches the end of the street and must stop. She falls: bump on her head, scraped elbow, bruised knee. Cheek pressed against the blacktop, she looks up the street to make sure her husband hasn't followed her. She doesn't want him to see this. She wrestles with the bike to get it off of her and stands up, then stands the bike up beside her. She looks back up the hill now, gets her right foot over the bar, but now she can't just cruise; she has to pedal the bike. She pushes off, gains a moment of balance, but the action of pedaling throws her from side to side into territory where falling is the only possibility. Every ten feet, she either catches herself with her right foot, or she falls. Beaten and bruised, she reaches her house. She turns the bike around and faces it back down the street. She glances at the window and yes, her husband is still there watching. She turns back to her task, wants to give him no sign of weakness. Down and up the street she goes like this over and over. Sometimes a neighbor stops to talk and offer help, but she waves them off. The sun drops behind the tops of trees and the neighborhood darkens. At her house, she turns the bike around and faces it down the hill. One more time, and then it'll be dark, and then she'll put up her bike and go inside and her husband will hold her and they'll cry together. It used to be that you could practice something and you would learn, you would get better. She prepares herself for this last trip down the hill. The air is cooler now and feels even better. She's up on the bike now, drifting, drifting. The cooler air penetrates her sweater and thrills her entire body. Now her bowed arms connecting to the handlebars at her hands truly feel like wings. The neighbors' houses glide past her. The tall pines sough and swing in the breeze. She reaches the end of the street, but it isn't the end. It just keeps going, and it's all down hill. Thank God, thank God, down hill and seemingly endless. She picks up speed, grows lighter, almost floating free of the earth. Buildings once full of light and people, but now abandoned and dark, fly by. Where is everybody? But some buildings are still well-lit and full of faces and dancing shadows. No time to stop, though, must keep going and going. Rivers wind past her. Lakes reflect the moon. She remembers swimming naked in them at night with her friends, and once with her lover. Great mountains rise up, high plains that go on forever. Horses that she has loved appear and bow to her. No, that's not right, she says, and bows instead to them. A drumbeat arises and the laughing faces of women encircle her. Her husband's face is there and he is speaking but she can't hear his words. Then it's just darkness and more darkness. It seems to deepen and widen, but it's okay. The darkness embraces and touches every part of her. She flies deeper and deeper into it. Her mind and heart grow clear as bells. They ring and ring in the distance. She doesn't know how but the darkness deepens and deepens, but it's truly okay, no it's better than okay, better and better. Sweeter. Then her husband's face is right there and she can hear his voice, but she doesn't understand the words. He lifts the bicycle off of her. She had forgotten it was there. He helps her to stand and holds her and holds her. It's okay, he says, it's okay. Yes, she repeats into his chest over and over again. It's okay, it's okay.

Witness

On that very morning when you are most
exhausted, maybe you'll be graced by the will to rise
and wake your dying wife for the long day.
The dog that slept between the two of you stretches
and yawns as if the world belongs to only her.
Your wife still drifts in the outskirts of her dreams,
whispering about the horse who escaped from the barn
and foundered in a neighbor's field ten years ago.

You draw the bedclothes away and she stirs, tries to grab
the sheet and pull it back, your first small tug-of-war
of the day. If you have been graced with that will
to be present, you let her win. The dog climbs
on her chest, licks her face, and she laughs and laughs.

You help her to sit up, turn her to bring her feet off
the bed, slide her to the edge and into your arms,
your first embrace of the day, her face against your chest,
yours against her tousled hair, a soft kiss, love
present in every touch. You help her
with the portable toilet, then bathe her, touching her
in all the places long-time lovers know.

You dress her, wrestling the shirt onto her lifeless
left arm. Sometimes she cries, without any new cause
you can see—a weeping deep and complete. And if
you are still here the way she is, the way the air

and the light are, you learn to witness without
weeping yourself, without retreating to another room
to stare out the window at whatever is still there.

The Bite

Sometimes
she resents
all my touching,
guiding, coaxing—how little
she can do for herself now,
this woman who could always
do so much.
When she can tolerate it
no longer,
she bites me—hard—
on the shoulder.
Ah, God, it hurts.
The bite itself, yes,
but it's another pain—shame,
or is it guilt? How
have I hurt her this time?
I lower her to her seat.
You bit me, I say.
That's right, she says,
and if you call me "Sweetie"
one more time,
I'll bite you again.

Her Walking

At first she walked on her own, sometimes for miles,
on the Black Water Creek trails. Then she began to get lost
and to wander, happily. Friends would run into her,
talk with her for a while, point her in the right direction,
then give me a worried call. Knowing her preferences,
I hiked out on the trail, found her, took her by the hand,
and led her home. How she loved to walk, to notice
the deer noticing her, rare fox flicking the bush
of its tail, dusk-arisen skunk hunting beetles and slugs,
hawk perched on a low limb so still in its looking
the wind treated it as stone, buzzards thrashing
their dark wings against thick, green leaves of a magnolia.

Later, she became tired sooner, and her walks grew
shorter and shorter. She used a cane, determined
to make it back to the forest trails, shuffling somehow
over roots and rocks. From somewhere out there, unable
to steal another step, she called me on her cell to come
get her, and quickly please. And I would drive my car
to the closest point and hike in to find her more like
a strange statue than the woman I loved, twisted
over her cane, her body tightened into a knot she couldn't
untie. I coaxed from her one troubled step after another
for half a mile to the street and our car. Neighbors
came out to see her and somehow she was happy,
cracking jokes and crying at the same time.

Later she walked just around the block, but even then
sometimes her body froze in the middle of the street
like a scarecrow traffic cop and the cars would ease
around her. Until her walks were just down to the corner
and back. She wanted to be on her own, to feel the wind
on her face, to feel the little animal surprises in the trees
and shrubs, to follow the river of her own thoughts without
somebody telling her what she couldn't do.

Now she walks with me on one side and Caitlyn on the other.
We help her stand from the wheelchair, ask her to point
her bellybutton to the street so she will stand up straight
and balance better. She laughs at the catbird, her favorite,
who covers every birdsong she will ever need to hear.
Then, I say, "Right foot," and she concentrates, exerts
an enormous effort, her right foot trembling, rising,
then landing on the concrete. In this way, we proceed,
coaxing her with "Right foot, left foot, right foot, left foot. . ."
the verbalization helping to pull some trigger in her mind.
In almost any weather the three of us walk together,
though to us it is really just she who is walking,
and we only part of the machinery of her moving,
intimate companions holding her close as we make
our way out and back the concrete path leading
to our front stoop and door. She cocks her head to listen
to the cardinal on the highest limb of the apple tree,
proclaims in a week she'll be jogging again. A great dream,
the two of us jogging together, hopping over roots and stones
on the path—calling the crazy wet dog back from the creek.

Pyramids

I needed to go to Walmart for a few things. Harriet was lying
on her couch, as usual. Just lying there, she was thinking too much
about everything, and her sadness was coming back. When I asked
her if she wanted to go to Walmart with me, she said, "Sure." So I
transferred her into her wheelchair, rolled her out to the car, drove
to Walmart, put her back in her wheel chair, rolled her through the
first barrier of automatic doors into the foyer. And that's when I
saw it: one of those drivable electric shopping carts with a basket on
the front. I rolled her next to it.

"What do you think," I said, "you want to drive this?"

She looked at me, and her eyes lit up. "Yeah!" she said.

So I settled her into the middle of the cushy seat, used her gait
belt to strap her in, showed her how to use the controls, little joy
sticks that she could push and pull. She tentatively drove the cart
toward the second barrier of automatic doors. This is going to
be great, I thought. When the door opened, she shot through it.
"Welcome to Walmart," someone to my left said, but I didn't have
time to be polite. Harriet had already turned right onto the first
main aisle of the store and was picking up speed. I jogged behind her
as best I could. "Slow down!" I yelled, but she couldn't hear me, or
was ignoring me. She picked up more speed. I was running now. The
row of cash registers was to our right, and I could see it dawning in
the eyes of customers in lines waiting to pay that Harriet was not
going to slow down. Their eyes grew even wider as she approached.
Some dropped their shopping bags that exploded onto the floor with
toothbrushes, garden trowels, and summer hats. The line split just
enough to let her fly through, and I rode her wake but had to leap
over a little girl reaching down for her brand new doll.

Ahead of Harriet now, people dove right and left for their lives,
throwing whatever they had in their hands into the air. I dodged the
fallout as it rained down spatulas, underwear, a hairdryer, and red and
green apples. She reached the grocery section and turned left toward
the back of the store. I glanced behind me and took note of the
mayhem but didn't have time to linger. I was running behind her as
fast as I could go. She veered right into the canned goods aisle and

took out a stacked pyramid of baked beans. A chaos of cans tumbled and rolled on the floor in front of me. I kicked as many out of the aisle as I could. When I looked up, she was gone. I heard screams from a distant part of the store. I ran down the aisle and turned left. I could see her flying along frozen foods at the westernmost wall. She was heading straight for a woman who casually browsed the coolers, oblivious. Slow down, Harriet, please slow down, I thought, as I ran. She did, but not enough, and ran right into the woman's butt. The woman jumped straight up in the air with a scream, turned and glared at Harriet. Harriet glared right back at her.

But no, when I got there, panting, they were both laughing. Even the woman's little boy sitting in their shopping basket was laughing.

"I'm so sorry," I said, "she just got away from me."

"It's alright," the woman said, still laughing, "no harm done."

"Thank God," I said.

Harriet's eyes were full of a profound glee.

"You keep leaving me," I said.

Her eyes shone in a way I hadn't seen in a long time. "Get over it," she said.

"I want you to stay close to me now," I said.

She looked at me and waggled her eyebrows maniacally as only she could. She pulled the left lever back and the cart backed up. Then she turned left, hit the throttle with her right hand, headed straight at me. I jumped out of the way as she whizzed by.

"Jesus!" I yelled.

"Christ!" she yelled as she turned a corner and disappeared.

I ran after her, but when I turned the same corner, I couldn't see her anywhere. Shouts and screams rose from a distant part of the store. When I arrived at the hardware section, several guys were lying on the floor with wrenches and work gloves scattered all around them, but strangely they were laughing.

I had to catch her before somebody got seriously hurt. I kept following the screams, but always arrived too late. Electronics, Household, Pharmacy, Lawn and Garden, always people strewn about and giggling at whatever had just happened. After a while, the shouts and screams got farther away, until finally they stopped. This was a huge Walmart store but I covered every inch of it three times looking for her. Not a restroom unexplored. No potted plant, bird feeder, or pet rock left unturned. Finally I spotted an employee in a red vest and khakis.

"How can I help you sir?"

"My wife," I said, "I've lost her."

"I'm sorry to hear that," she said.

"She's in an electric cart," I said, "and she just disappeared."

"Oh, that explains it," she said. "These new carts of ours are now equipped with warp drive."

"What?" I said.

"Yeah," she said, "your wife could be anywhere in the universe. But when the batteries start getting low, she'll have to return."

"That's good to know," I said.

"Just be patient," she said. "Why don't you take a nap in our furniture section?"

She pointed toward a huge yellow lounge chair. A large sign saying "Try me" was pinned to it. So I did. I sat in that chair, raised my feet, put my hands behind my head, and stared at the Walmart ceiling, which looked amazingly like a clear white infinite sky. In fact, there were birds up there flying among the cross beams, sparrows I believe. My mind took a leap. I imagined Harriet somewhere out there in the universe dodging the stars at warp speed.

When I woke up, Harriet was sitting next to me in her cart. Her brow was furrowed. She mock-pouted. "Out of juice," she said.

"It happens to the best of us," I said. But then she smiled.

"What is it?" I asked.

"I've gotta have one of these things. It makes everything come close." She pointed toward the sporting goods section. She was seeing some far-away place in her mind. After a moment, her hand floated down to her lap.

"Did you know at the speed of light, time stops?" she asked.

"I didn't," I said.

"Nothing moves," she said, "Everything just is. I saw it all. I saw what is."

"What do you mean, 'what is,'" I said. She brightened and looked up at me, waggling her eyebrows. "I will never die," she said. "Nobody ever really dies."

I let that stand for a moment, watched her seeing it, not wanting her not to see it. Her eyes softened. She said, nodding her head, "Harriet will die. But I won't."

I didn't know what to say to that, partly because I wasn't sure what she meant. It was getting late. I needed to go back to the entrance and retrieve her wheelchair. One thing was for sure: that cart wasn't going anywhere. We still had some things we needed to buy. I could see her sadness coming back.

"Did you know," I said, "you took out a pyramid of baked beans in that thing?"

"Yes," she said, "that's not the only pyramid I took out." And then she laughed and laughed. So did I. Walmart shoppers of every stripe just stared at us. We didn't care. Pyramids were falling everywhere.

The Hills

I don't know what comes after death.
It could be the nothingness of deep sleep.
Or the strange orientation to time and space
of dreams. Or a dimension I can't fathom
with words, or imagine with my senses.

But I do know that something in me
has awakened, jumped the rails and headed
for the hills. I know she lives there waiting
for me. As she becomes wordless in this world,
she communicates more and more in that one.
She wanders fearless and amazed among those
endless trails. I know she is not her wounded
brain, not her failing body, not the impasses
her doctors and healers define her by.
Sometimes I have taken that leap and I'm in
the hills with her. If there are words there,
they are the essences of words, never stepping
into form—all its suffering and fear.

Banana Pudding

When you would eat nothing else,
you would eat Camille's banana pudding.
She really knows how to make it.
Not the salmon, not the green beans,

not the asparagus, not the broccoli,
no matter how carefully I prepared them.
But you would eat that banana pudding.
You dipped your spoon into it slowly,

pulled it out when you had a perfect bite
and held it for a moment before your gaze,
equal parts banana, pudding, and meringue.
You slid it into your mouth like cautiously

parking a small boat into a slip. You allowed
it to stay there for a moment, and the pain
withdrew from your face, and something
like a smile, an expression of ecstasy,

took its place. The spoon slipped back out
clean as a whistle, but the bite dwelled
in your mouth for a while until you chewed
with your eyes closed and finally swallowed.

Mmmm you said, nodding your head,
opening your eyes to look at me in wonder.
And there was more, thank God. I wanted
it to last forever. And thank God

Camille kept coming, every couple
of weeks, with a still-warm-from-the-oven
banana pudding. Until those last days, when
even that was impossible for you to eat, the last

of the sweet pleasures of this old world.

The Feather

Her anger rises sometimes to the surface
with a threatening glare and sharp voice.
The bait I cast out there is my impatience,
my urgency to control, my unconscious
condescension. If there is bliss
in this abyss, it's as fleeting as a wren's
feather in a storm—unlike our shaman's
Condor feather, sturdy as a branch
of Ironwood, acquired during our days
with a shaman in the mountains of Peru.
I stroke it over her body and over mine
to collect the dark energy—radiation, chemo,
bathroom visits turned horror show—
then flick it away in the air where it dies.
Cleanse me, heal me, teach me—the prayer
the shaman taught us. Even after all
these years, we need that shaman's feather
to keep the darkness moving away so we can
find each other where we always have been,
always are, right here, right now.

The Minutes

At night sometimes I study your sleeping
silhouette. I pray that your sleep

is so deep that you leave all form
behind, all history, all memory of what

you built in this life and then gave up
like tidal waters receding from the sand.

I study the face that I have touched,
that I have pressed with my own face,

that I have kissed ten thousand times.
It's hard to say what I learn

from such attention, my mind sunk
into stillness, my heart hung on the hook

of your slow, steady breathing. Maybe
I understand more deeply the frailness

of the body, and the presence of a light
burning inside that keeps you wanting

to live, to taste, to hear, to see. Unable
to turn over on your own, to get up

and go to the toilet without my help,
you will sleep on your back all night.

Our small dog lies belly up between us,
snoring, one paw flicking at the sight

of a disappearing deer. Like you she loves
to run, to chase the white-tailed mysteries

until she's lost, stopped in her tracks.
Then the fun begins, navigating sometimes

to my high-pitched whistle, finding her
way back. I turn on my side to face the wall,

wishing I had some magical call that would
bring you home from the deepest woods

you've ever known. The bedside table, stacked
with partially read books, presents the face

of the digital clock, manifesting, patiently,
the white number of each eternal minute.

The Scheme

This is almost too simple for words.
She had
a few days left to live. In our living room
she lay
on the hospital bed, TV on, but the sound
was off,
an ancient, rowdy episode of *Mash*—
helicopters landing,
the wounded carried on stretchers
to the OR,
Hawkeye and BJ up to no good, ogling
Hot Lips,
tormenting Frank and Colonel Potter,
enlisting
Radar in yet another doomed scheme.
But she wasn't
watching TV anymore. Her eyes were
mostly closed
and when they opened they didn't look
at me,
or anyone, just stared. This was before
the night
of death rattles. This was before
the nurse
told me to stop trying to feed her, to give her
water.
I was sitting in a chair beside her bed,
facing her,
right hand on top of her right hand.
I asked her
if she could look at me just one more time.
She turned
her head (at what cost!) slightly toward me,
opened
her eyes, searched for mine, found them,

held the gaze
for a moment. There you are, I said.
Slight nod.
We need ole Hawkeye to help us with a scheme,
I said.
The tiny wren of a smile perched for a moment
on her lips
before flitting away. She loved that big-hearted
rascal.
He'd kept her laughing, kept her company,
on many
of those long, horizontal days. She reached
the limit
of her strength, closed her eyes, let her head roll
against the pillow.
I moved closer to her face. "I love you," I said.
She summoned
her strength and whispered "I love you,"
the last words
she ever spoke to anyone, like the sound
of a fine-point pen
flying on paper, a burning scar on my heart—
the last,
best, craziest scheme we ever hatched
together.

Everything

You have done it all
There is nothing left to do
You can let go now

Let go of your eyes
that have seen too much
and too little,
your hands that have played
the strings, the keys,
the skins of animals
stretched tight over the drums

Let go of the horses,
the loving of them,
the training, riding them
to victories and losses,
standing with them
in midnight pastures
full of cool breezes

Let go of your face
you pressed so often
into your own hands

your tongue that loved
the taste of food,
the taste of words

your voice
that rode the breath
of your songs

Let go of your knees, elbows,
shoulders, belly, genitals,
and your feet
no need to stand on them
or see them or touch them again

Let go of your friends
and your enemies,
your mother and father,
your brothers and sisters,
the assorted smiles you gave them

Let go of your mind
its thoughts and beliefs
Let go of every one of them
They won't help you now

Let go of your dog
who lies at the foot of your bed
studying every labored breath you take

Let go of me
who sits beside you
holding your right hand
these words
falling out of me like leaves
I love you
I know you love me

Everything has been said
except this
Do not be distracted
by anything
Go to the light

And this
Be at peace
You are ready now

You have let it all go
Nothing can hold you
to this place any more

People of Chalk

Two old men arrived cracking jokes.
They were ordinary men
on a day for them like any other,
retrieving bodies, driving them
to the funeral home, the crematorium.
I had not anticipated the pain
of seeing them slide you
from hospice bed to gurney,
wheel you out the front door and to the street
where they loaded you into the back
of their van. I had not anticipated
that moment of realizing
I would never lay eyes on you again,
a banishment of sorts.

Your final chauffeurs, they drove you
that day across town. I know
you saw nothing from the windows,
no ornamental cherry trees
in their late September gloom.
No orange cat poking its head up
from the leaves as you pass by.
No crows gathered in the crown of an old tree
to make their raucous choir.
Not even those children clutching their thick
cylinders of chalk to draw grids
for their games, colorful dancing
characters in the sidewalk frames.

3. The Banishment of With and Without

Whirlwind

For Harriet in the Bardo

I empty my heart but the husk is hard
I empty my mind but the body will not let go
of the way your flame carries on
in the emptiness of my rooms

if it were up to me
I would set you onto me again
you who have your own potent ghosts
a host of follower flames
that would keep me burning for years

while I sleep you are climbing a mountain
running your hands over the flowers
catching a glimpse of deer
that graze on those precipitous slopes

for a few days you walk alone
you let the rain come to you
your ghosts disintegrate
in the cold mountain streams
but your flame deepens like a rose

I know you won't return to me
I try not to be greedy
I savor the small fragrance of your hair
that remains
though it burns in my nostrils
like ripened dust

I must not suffer the loss of you
for the rest of my life
I must turn to other people
must test the scope of my heart

while what was once near
that I would still hold

rises up in a whirlwind of leaves
for just a moment

Gone

The more gone you are, the more
you're gone. I live alone. I hear

the clock, the compressor pushing air,
my own breath moving through nostrils,

the repertoire of the catbird, the dog
rolling over on the hardwood floor.

I can barely imagine sex, barely imagine
love as I knew it. Looking inward

I find the nothing there.
I pay the bills, I cook, see friends,

seek the center of my being that both
is and isn't me. I don't mean to speak

in riddles. In your absence, I pursue God
who is and isn't me, is and isn't

everything I see, is and isn't the nothing
from which it all emerges and into which

it all disappears. As if such a God
could ever be found. Your ashes

are scattered on the ground,
are blended into the clay pottery

of your friend, have settled in a silver
urn encircled with birds in flight.

What You Left Behind in the Silent House

for Harriet (1951-2016)

1

Given as get-well gifts for you,
three birds perch in a row
atop a Boze speaker, each
made of polyester fiber and stuffed
with polyethylene pellets.

The chickadee, white-chested,
light blue back
and wings, shock of genius
conductor hair standing
straight up on top of its head,

blurts four curling happy notes
again and again when I press
its back with my thumb. The cardinal,
red with a black mask face
chirps "purdy purdy purdy"

and your dog, my dog now, turns
to stare. The bobolink, black
and white with a yellow patch
on the back of its head, scratches
out a mad proliferation of notes

somehow always returning
to a strangely melodious theme.
Three more of these perch
somewhere downstairs
in the storage room shadows

silent as the forgotten song
of an old, worn-out record.
I could bring them up to the light,
get them all started at once,
a wild cacophonous choir

singing and raving, raging
against the silence of this house.

2

An upright Knabe piano in the corner. On the music stand,
a stained-glass owl you made in an arts and crafts class years ago.

A fat brown notebook crammed full of songs from famous
musicals and singer-songwriters. A 1928 illustrated edition

of Louisa May Alcott's *An Old-Fashioned Girl*. On the top lid,
a glass paperweight, half a globe, and within, a hand amid

foliage, apricot in its palm. Or is it a heart grown ripe and freshly
picked? A Capitol No. 45 clock made by the William L. Gilbert

Clock Company, the pendulum medallion presenting a portrait
of an unknown woman. A Matryoshka doll, woman within

woman within woman, reminding me of you, and you, and you.
A gold adjustable lamp leans over the music. And finally, a hinged gold

double frame containing photos of you and of me age seven, me
with flat-top and grin, you with blond hair just covering the ears,

short bangs, and that enigmatic smile. If I close the frames, we are eye
to eye, lip to lip, apricot to apricot, and the piano, silent, accumulates dust,

waiting for your hands to gather over the keys, and begin again.

3

Photographs. Some of them of you or me
or us, like the one with you in your boots
and breeches and me in the black leather jacket,
striding, grinning as if nothing bad in the world
could ever touch us. Or the one with me relaxing
on the recliner and you sitting on top of me as if I
were the chair, our corgi Dylan Thomas lying back
in your lap. But there are these other ones, your

experiments, like the one of a huge driftwood trunk
stretched out on the beach, two thick branches reaching
like the gaping jaws of some heretofore unknown
beast, and lying on the tongue of that toothless maw
like a blazing piece of candy, the bright yellow sun
of dawn or dusk, I'm no longer certain which,
half buried in that edgeless line of horizon
among auras of pink and gold.

Or like the one of me, though unrecognizably so,
shot from behind on the beach, brilliant full moon
breaking through gray clouds low on the horizon,
laying down a perfect white path directly to my feet,
my body a black silhouette against the dappled whiteness
of that trail, arms stretched out like wings, but I never
take the leap, never walk on the water,
eternally stuck in the wet sand like Keats's lover
straining unrequited on the Grecian urn.

Or the one of a dark-skinned Peruvian child
in a high mountain pass, dressed in thick clothes to combat
the cold wind and carrying a white lamb in his arms
across the boulder-strewn tundra, whether to heal
some minor lameness or for the slaughter, I will never know.

And look at this last one, taken through a glass globe that holds the sage and stripped trees of the Wyoming plains upside down. The right-side-up world beyond is blurred out of focus: upside-down clarity within right-side-up confusion. Your eye is always finding through the camera what is there, and something else: a palimpsest—the essential lying just beneath it all.

4

Stars. When we first moved into this house
twenty-five years ago, you attached white
phosphorescent stars of different sizes
to the ceiling and walls of our bedroom.
Tonight, when I turn out the light for sleep,
I'm surrounded by this likeness of a cloudless
night sky. When I awaken in the middle
of darkness, your invented constellations
tell the archetypal tales of our forty-five
years together with cat and dog and horse.
Your showers of shooting stars never move
an inch, summoning a stillness I don't want
to escape. I sleep, captured in your light.

5

Musical instruments everywhere. Your life-long guitar
in its case, missing strings but still alert, its potential
clinging to the polished wood. Banjo, fiddle, dulcimer,

ukulele. In a corner behind a door like our never-child
hiding from her mother, a cello you acquired just before
your diagnosis, and never played. It too is waiting,

wondering what spirit will inhabit it next. Three
kalimbas (aka thumb pianos), two sets of bongos, half
a dozen harmonicas scattered around the shelves

and drawers of this house. Two djembes, one yours,
one mine. You taught me the rhythms and we played,
the long trance of the beat holding us, leading us to

discoveries ripening in our hands until we stopped
together, on the same strike—one mind, one heart.
Presence—or was it absence—enveloped us.

Many flutes, but especially four Native American ones, one
you played slowly and mournfully at your mother's
funeral. One for me, and we played these together too,

you teaching me how to hold the drone while you explored,
and then you held the drone, my turn to fly and flourish.
The music itself, still moving through this body, the song

rhyming and refraining, the story unfolding, the life.

6

Vivid dreams, almost every night.
Occurring in complicated, undulating
landscapes with great vistas and forests,
canyons, rivers, fiercely blue skies streaked
by white vapor trails. Sometimes gargantuan
houses, convoluted hallways and staircases

leading to bedrooms with the covers pulled
back and waiting, dining rooms with chandeliers
hanging low, studies crammed to the ceiling
with books, playrooms with pool tables, all
populated by strangers who want to keep me
from catching up to you. I follow you into

a long, cold basement with narrow, ground level
windows looking out on passing feet,
roots bubbling up to the surface, leaves
tumbling like rolled dice. Whether in house
or landscape you are inscrutable, elusive.
You speak, but I can't understand

the strange, new language on your tongue.
I can tell you are no longer interested
in the likes of me, the museum of this house.
Driven by some purpose beyond mind,
you jump up suddenly to spring
through a door, leap over a fence, merge

with the trees, multiplying in your disappearance
like the fall leaves. I chase after you, feeling
there was something else that needed
to be said, always something else. But
as in life you are light and nimble, quick
as a red fox, the splash of your yellow hair

here and there, and then gone. I find myself
alone on swinging bridges over windy canyons,
in caves that grow smaller and smaller
until my body will not pass through.
The long way back is in absolute darkness.
Though I might speak of it here, in my dreams

I haven't thought yet to simply
let you go, to remain seated on the spot
where you have left me and feel the wind
on my skin, sunlight slip-sliding through
the canopies of maple and cherry, playing its music
on me with hands made of light and shadow.

7

The owl you drew in colorful chalk
hung from the mantelpiece with tape.
It flies out of the night sky swirling
with the auras of stars, out of the dark

face of the moon eclipsed by your winged
body, round white eyes looking
through me to something else far away—
I am the silence of this house.

Here

In that lost forest and field near
the broken-down bank of the dam
that kept the spring rains back
for half of one summer only
before the yellow sand and red clay

lunged across the feet of loblolly pines
that burst into needles above the heads
of young oaks and maples; in that
first forest of our time alone together,
I return now with our old but still

spirited corgi, on a cool April afternoon,
the giant spring buds of storm clouds
huddling overhead. I stand in the grass
where we first touched, where our eyes
first held without fear of time or silence.

Here the sand still fingers out into grass,
palms the earth and holds it beneath us,
and here the empty reservoir still gapes
against the summer sky, where for weeks
we swam in the first skins of our affections,

where the fish grew bold if we didn't keep
moving, so we kept moving. Back then
the bottom was firm clean sand, now
clogged with thorns and young trees
that won't survive. If you were here

you'd say not everything *should* survive,
and you'd be right, of course. Right
as our corgi returning from the woods,
running wild in her unaccustomed freedom,
dropping old bones on the ground before me.

The Drums

Years before the ice moon
rose in your brain, the women came
with drums, made a circle in our living room,
and you led them in the ancient rhythms
you had learned first from an old man
who knew the way and the reasons why,
and from the women too who already knew.

You just kept learning until they made you
their leader. You loved them and they loved you
and the sound of drums made the whole house
shake and the neighbors wonder. I retreated

to my room and listened to the laughter
and the beat, felt my heart being tuned
to a frequency sweeter than the one
the day had made of me, sweeter than the one
the long procession of days and years
had made of me. The burden of my grudges

and greed fell away like loosened masks.
When the women left, you came to find me,
drew me into the room we shared.
We lay down together without the obstructions
of thought and habit and fell into the emptiness
of each other's eyes where soundless drums
woke us up from our long and heavy dream of each other.

After the ice moon rose in your brain
and you could no longer use your hands
for drumming, the women kept coming
anyway, drumming and laughing, lifting you
out of the body no longer good for walking
or feeding itself or driving a car or reading a book—

lifting you out of the mind no longer good
for remembering the day we climbed to the peak
of Sharp Top Mountain, the day we made love
on the cool, blue, back porch, woodpeckers
beating their drums, filling the neighborhood
with their calls to mates that were always answered.

"Two of them,"

I said. "Yes," you said, smiling,
"but which two?" That caught me
off guard, as your words often did.

It never occurred to me that you
knew specific pairs of pileated
woodpeckers. We often heard them,

one answering from a distance,
one clinging to the other side
of a nearby tree, its head

popping into view to check us out.
We two humans hear their song
as laughter, at first mechanical

and even maniacal. But then
it isn't, containing multitudes
of subtle layers from raucous

to tender. The field guides
call them shy, but once we saw
a male not ten feet from us, standing

atop a dead log as if he had felled it.
He was hammering purposefully,
cutting away bark to get to something

good—carpenter ants, scattering
wildly now in their own panicked world.
He glanced at us and cocked his head,

brown bead of an eye embedded
in a black stripe on his white face,
red crest a smokeless flame.

His mate called from some tree a hundred
yards away, drawing closer, finally
peering down at us from a high limb.

But a day came when there was no she
to *us* two, and I came here alone to offer
some of your ashes to the woods. Who knew

it was possible to love cold ashes,
and to know where they belong,
here, with a particular pair of pileated

woodpeckers playing, swooping
through the trees overhead, working
as a team. A strange rain of bark

and slivers of wood fall into the dead leaves
all around me, to join the small
white pieces of bone and ash.

A Man

One winter years before you died,
the snow and ice were so deep and durable
you had plenty of time for house-bound
projects—building a ramp for the dog,
a wooden trunk for storing our games.
One day you strode into the room
and ceremoniously placed a floppy blue
knitted hat on my head—a little too big
and a lot too loose. It felt right, though,
coming off your hands onto me. It might

fall off me any minute in the wind,
but I know how to kneel down and pick
it up. So even on freezing days when
I forget it in the drawer, because you spent
those long hours making it for me, my head
remembers its warmth, recalls the click
of your needles, the humming of tunes,
and your happiness with the dog
lying on your foot. The soul cannot
be proven, while bone and blood

return to dust and fly among the clouds.
On our table there was food and drink,
the possibility of hand touching hand,
laughter over the lack of flavor in the meat,
the savory tartness of red raspberry pie.
So I will not complain about your wobbly hat,
but wear it with a large pin to hold it on.
I want to be a man who doesn't whine about his losses,
but talks about the way the day is present to him,
and he to it, exploring the cold wind with a good hat.

The Banished

I sit on the side porch drinking strong coffee and reading a wisdom book. We used to read them together and discuss. "I get it, but I don't agree," you'd say, and off we'd go. A long train groans on the tracks nearby. A siren whines in the distance. Five sparrows cling to the yellow feeder, with lots of chirping from surrounding foliage. Fall leaves, red and yellow, shuffle in the trees and on the damp ground. The string of bells you hung from a limb jingles.

Our corgi curls up near my left foot, listening, I think, to the rough call of a crow. Cicadas, frogs, and crickets maintain a constant whir. A cardinal lights on the head of St. Francis, turns and turns, bobs and cocks his head, looking for his companion, flickering, I think, in the azaleas. So strange that you are not here.

The emptiness threatens to suck everything named and unnamed into it, leaving me with nothing but an unruffled membrane of awareness. The heaviness of the train bearing down on steel rails has passed. A chainsaw grumbles from somewhere deep in the nearby woods. As the breeze rises, your chimes have a turn. They find a pattern, a strangely discordant tune.

Another fat, scruffy cardinal lands on a limb just a few feet away. Cocks its head every which way to look at me. Hops sideways on the limb to get closer. Can the eyes of a human meet the eyes of a bird? A thought hops into me that it's you come back this way just to say hello. Stupid thought, but I allow it. What is it that travels the trail from eye to eye? Does it enter me, or I, it? Slipping back and forth, watching in both directions. Break one boundary and the immense energy and frailty of the other manifests. I am a scruffle of feathers and hollow bones shot through with lightning alertness. I am thoughtless intimacy with air.

Our corgi pretends to be asleep, one eye open, ready to pounce whenever a squirrel makes a move. Crazy little dog who loves to chase but not to catch.

No me or you or we or us, but all of it all at once. Outside and inside, the same. I can neither have you nor lose you. With and without are banished forever.

Whirlpool

Those years ago, I almost lost you in the white
water of the New River Gorge. Our guide
looked over at us and shouted, "We can
swim this part. Follow me." He slipped
from the side of the raft and disappeared,

head surfacing again twenty feet away.
He motioned for us to follow, and so we did,
climbed over the side, let go of it, caught now
in the river's current that carried us like otters
through sluices and over stone tables,

holding us back before slingshotting us
forward, our bodies slithering through
the murky passages. Then I felt you pulled
from me into a different current, skimming
on your back over a round boulder feet

first into a whirlpool waiting on the other side.
It swallowed you whole. You were gone
and didn't come back up. I was too far past,
scrambling upstream to reach you. The guide
saw you, got there fast, and pulled you out.

You rested on the bank, eyes wide, coughing.
"It spun me around and around," you said.
"It wasn't going to let me go." You looked a little
different out of your eyes from that day on,
knowing you didn't know what would happen next.

No Wonder

You know the horse you ride
the way a painter intuits hues
of merging colors, the way a sculptor
feels in her curled hand the sinew
of wood or stone, the way a writer
invites wayward words
to perch on a branch in her brain.

You ride deep in the saddle, balanced,
hands on the reins in ready contact
with his sensitive mouth, allowing
his head and neck to reach out,
relaxed, muscles flowing, ears alert
and forward, your legs bowed
to the flanks, eyes focused ahead

on the forest trail or the open field
seeking an obstacle—a wall, a fence,
a gully—to fly across, hooves churning
beneath you like cogs in the wheel of earth,

your eyes turning also inward, drawing
some essence of yourself down
into the core of that giant, a place
devoid of time or space, bereft
of thoughts and words, barren and crowded
all at once, full of thundering muscle and bone,
the smoke of burning breath, the hiss
of ripped air, the fusion of two into one.

No wonder you don't want to come down
from there, riding all day and all night,
sun transforming into moon, clouds
into black sky and fiery stars. No wonder
you want never to come back.

Epilogue

Towheaded Thrower of Stones (2)

Years later, the towheaded thrower of stones
returns to the muscular branch of her childhood tree.
She has gathered stones that caught her eye—

talismans—from the Montana Rockies,
the castle ruins of Wales, the Costa Rican
cloud forests, the Peruvian confluences of rivers,

the stone-infested coastline of Nova Scotia—
and brought them here in her box. She turns
each one over and over in her hand, listening

closely to its small voice as innocent as the eye
of a crow. Through gaps in the canopy she throws
each one in its time. She knows she will never

again see this old oak split once by lightning, base
of the trunk half hollow, half still pushing the sap.
One stone wants to be an artist whose paintings

bring this grieving world to a halt.
One demands to be an unbroken horse
swimming cold, fast-running rivers, jumping

the stupid fences of men, climbing boulder-filled
canyons, carrying a rider as fearless as the eye
of a rogue bear. One begs to be the backsliding

preacher of an old country church, wants to drink
himself wild and weeping under the fatherless
night sky. One wants to be a tap dancer with top hat

and cane cavorting on a stage before thousands.
This towheaded stone-thrower cannot
tell the stones what they should want, how far

they should fly, what life they should live. The word
"should" is banished from her mind. All she can do
is throw and watch them vanish in the distance

like almost everyone else she has ever known.
One stone gazes up at her from the box, wants to be
a crone tending to her garden and trees, remembering

that foolish old man who planned to be here with her.
The final stone wants to die and come back to life, wants
to keep on dying and coming back as someone dark

or full of light, someone cracked and crazy or balanced
as a worldly saint. The stone-thrower holds this one
for a long time in her palm and kisses it, as if

luck could be summoned by love or affection.
She looks out through the millions of leaves flickering
in the late light like all the stones she has ever thrown.

She lets the last one go and it flies far away, landing
on the dark floor of a forest, or of a troubled home, she
cannot tell. She can see, but she cannot look.

It's done, she says to the dying light, to the old tree still
twisting itself up against the sky, satisfied that her wildest
dreams of being are wreaking holy havoc in this world.

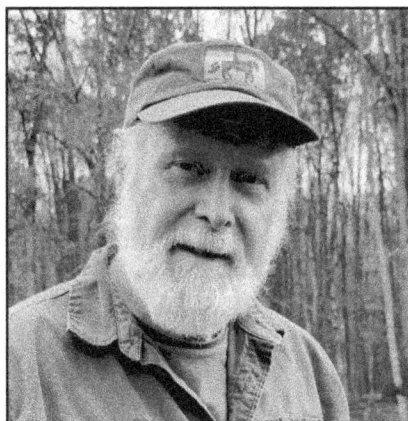

Towheaded Stone Thrower is Peterson's tenth book, which includes eight collections of poetry, a novel, and a collection of short stories. His most recent books are *The Sadness of Whirlwinds* (stories, 2021), *The Horse Who Bears Me Away* (poems, 2020), and *Speech Minus Applause* (poems, 2019). Hundreds of his poems and stories have been published in more than eighty journals. Peterson and his wife Harriet were together for 45 years. She died in September of 2016. Her long career as a professional equestrian (teaching, training, competing) broadened and deeply informed Peterson's life as a human being and a writer. His poems have won the Benjamin Saltman Award from Red Hen Press, an Academy of American Poets Award, and a Fellowship in Poetry from the Virginia Arts Commission. A number of his plays have been produced in regional and college theaters. Until his retirement in 2013, he was Coordinator of Creative Writing at Randolph College and was later the Pearl S. Buck Writer-in-Residence there in the Fall of 2017. Many years ago, he was founder and editor of the poetry journal Kudzu and later was editor of The Devil's Millhopper poetry magazine and press. He also taught for fifteen years in the University of Nebraska Omaha Low-Res MFA Program in Creative Writing. Born in Georgia and reared in South Carolina, he continues to live and write in the mysterious and beautiful foothills of southwest Virginia.

www.ingramcontent.com/pod-product-compliance
Lightning Source LLC
Chambersburg PA
CBHW021407090426
42742CB00009B/1045